On the table

The little car

is on the table.

The little doll

is on the table.

The little boat

is on the table.

The little truck

is on the table.

The little ball

is on the table.

The little plane

is on the table.

The little bus

is on the table.

The teddy bear is on the table.